How to Conduct Successful Meetings

A Step by Step Guide to Conducting a Successful Business Meeting

I0462868

By Meir Liraz

Published by BizMove
www.bizmove.com

Table of Contents

MEIR LIRAZ

1. Introduction

Was your last meeting successful? Were you an effective chairman or an active participant? Were those who had a contribution to make invited? Did the meeting accomplish the stated purpose? These questions and many more need to be asked and answered affirmatively if organizational meetings are to be successful. The chairman - the one who plans, hosts, and leads a meeting - must establish a proper environment. The environment, and the feeling conveyed to the participants by the chairman, will have a great impact on the outcome of the meeting. The chairman must stimulate, guide, clarify, control, summarize, and evaluate the discussion, keeping in mind his responsibility to accomplish the meeting objectives. If   he fails to perform his role effectively, the meeting may turn into meaningless discussions of irrelevant subjects, a series of pointless power plays, and even boring monologues.

Meetings are essential and can serve as an effective method of communication within an organization. They have been rightfully categorized by some managers as time-consuming, high-priced, and unproductive, but this need not be the case.

Sometimes we expect too much from a meeting. When it fails to meet our expectations, we may be too quick to criticize. William E. Utterback, author of Group Thinking and Conference Leadership, said, "It must not be supposed that the conference table possesses the magic property of generating wisdom when rubbed simultaneously by a dozen pairs of elbows." Meetings are helpful means of achieving coordination. When there is a gathering of people with a mutual interest, the results may be as follows:

Encourage participation in the subject of concern;

Integrate interests;

Broaden perspectives and change attitudes;

Improve decision-making; and

Motivate and commit participants to courses of action.

The fundamental decision concerning meetings is not whether to hold them, but how to make them effective. Recent studies show that members of middle management spend 30 percent of their time in meetings. Unproductive meetings can result in substantial loss to an organization.

On the other hand, a productive meeting becomes a tool for effective management communication, and serves as a vehicle for development of specific plans or the organization of specific tasks. In any case, successful meetings don't just happen; they occur as a result of careful planning, good leadership, and close attention to details before, during, and after the session.

2. The Planning Process

The key steps to be taken by the chairman in planning a meeting are as follows:

Establish the meeting objectives;

Prepare the meeting agenda;

Determine timing and physical arrangements;

Identify and invite participants; and

Consider matters of protocol.

Let's review each of these steps in detail.

Meeting Objectives

Why is the meeting being held? What will it accomplish? Meetings are usually held for one or more of the following reasons:

To disseminate new information or provide feedback;

To receive a report;

To coordinate efforts of a specific nature and obtain group support;

To win acceptance for a new idea, plan, or system;

To reconcile a conflict;

To negotiate an agreement;

To motivate members of a group;

To initiate creative thinking within a group; and

To solve a current problem within a group.

The meeting plan should not be too broad or the meeting may be doomed from the beginning.

Therefore, a wise chairman identifies realistic objectives for the meeting and is prepared to meet them.

Meeting Agenda

Is an agenda necessary? How long will it require to carry out the agenda? Would the meeting run smoothly and be just as successful without it?

The agenda should crystallize the intended meeting objective(s) and establish the time available to accomplish them. Whether the agenda is in writing or stated verbally by the chairman, it provides the framework to keep the meeting on target. Furthermore, it permits the chairman to devote his attention to managing the interplay of the participants.

The meeting should focus on the objective(s) and also on reaching the objective(s) in a pre-established, finite time schedule. Meetings that exceed established time limits usually are not constructive because opinions begin to replace facts. Such meetings are apt to go astray and may even disintegrate into personal contests or power plays between participants. There are several other points to consider during preparation of the agenda. Notable among them are:

Focus the agenda on items relating to the same general topic, if possible. Begin with a discussion of topics of major concern to participants; then, if necessary, discuss related topics of lesser importance. A meeting of this type requires fewer attendees and generates better participation in the discussion.

Schedule fewer agenda items when the topics cannot be related. It is difficult for most participants to come to a meeting completely prepared on a wide variety of topics. The more concise the agenda, the better.

Attach background data for each topic to be

discussed, when the agenda is distributed. This will ensure that each participant has some familiarity with the items before arriving at the meeting.

Establish a time limit and priority for each agenda item. Consider whether the topic to be discussed is familiar, new, controversial, or complex.

Don't have the meeting run too long. One hour is usually the norm for busy middle- to upper-level managers. When the meeting is scheduled on a quarterly, semiannual, or annual basis, it may run longer to accomplish the objectives. Schedule a "break" when the meeting is expected to take over 2 hours.

Submit the agenda to the participants, with the background data, as early as possible. This will give each participant more time to prepare for the meeting.

The chairman should be sure the meeting is needed. If the need disappears, he should cancel the meeting.

Time/Physical Arrangements

When should the meeting be held? Where should it

be held? There are several necessary considerations regarding time and physical arrangements for the meeting. Among the more important are:

The convenience of the place.

The size of the room. It should not be too large or too small. If the right-size room is not available, it is better to select a small room, rather than too large a room. A small room presents a friendlier atmosphere than a large, sparsely filled one.

The seating arrangement and the availability of extra seats if needed.

The lighting, heating, and ventilation.

Any visual aids required and their proper use.

Availability of extra paper and pencils.

The need for name plates or name tags.

The handling of messages.

It is the chairman's responsibility to begin and end the meeting on time. It is the responsibility of at-tendees to arrive on time. Two techniques proved effective in curing cases of chronic tardiness are (1) to ignore latecomers; and (2) to make no attempt to bring late-comers up to date.

Meeting Size

How many persons should be invited to the meeting? What is the purpose of inviting each person? The attendees should be viewed as management resources - each able to contribute to the meeting through knowledge or experience or both. It is wise to include some of the persons in the organization to whom action items may be given after the meeting. This tends to encourage better support for the topics to be discussed. Attendance by disinterested persons tends to increase non-relevant discussion and impede the meeting. Thus, the chairman should invite as many people as necessary, but no more.

The size of the meeting tends to affect the way it functions. For example, if attendance exceeds seven, there is a tendency for communication to become more centralized, and participants have less opportunity to communicate directly with one another. As the number of people invited increases, the ability of the chairman to predict the interaction that will take place becomes more difficult.

It is important to have all relevant points of view on

a particular subject under consideration represented at the meeting, even if this makes it a large meeting. A large meeting requires increased formality and extra time for each topic to ensure adequate communication between participants.

Proponents of the "small group" theory consider seven to be the maximum number of participants for a productive meeting. However, if a problem-solving type of meeting is to be held, some authorities claim that up to 12 participants can be accommodated effectively. If the number of participants exceeds 18, the chairman may find it almost impossible to accomplish the meeting objectives.

On the other hand, in a meeting involving only three participants, there may be a tendency for two of them to form a combination against the third participant. This could be disastrous so managers should guard against organizing too small a meeting.

Matters Of Protocol

Why should the chairman be concerned about protocol? How can this affect the success of a meeting? One of the initial steps to ensure a successful meeting is to give adequate consideration to protocol. Protocol might be defined as the application of common-sense courtesy.

Some steps the chairman might take to avoid protocol problems are:

Notify participants well in advance of the meeting date, and provide them with an agenda and background data.

Notify department heads when subordinates with expertise are needed.

Make sure that arrangements with resource persons outside the organization are completed before the meeting.

Introduce resource persons and newcomers at the start of the meeting. Also, make their affiliations and expertise known to the other attendees.

List participants in alphabetical order in the meeting announcement and minutes, unless someone present far outranks the others. In that case, list this person first.

Express gratitude to those from outside the group as well as to those within the group for significant contributions to the success of the meeting.

Advise those invited to attend the meeting of postponement or cancellation as far in advance as possible.

3. Running the Meeting

The chairman should make the meeting as relaxed and informal as possible. He should resort to Robert's Rules of Order only when attendance is large or debate becomes heated. The chairman should "manage" the meeting, speak when appropriate, encourage discussion, seek a consensus, and summarize. Under no circumstances should the chairman be unprepared, "hog" the discussion, play the comic, chastise a participant, or let the meeting run by itself.

The meeting will not get off the ground unless the participants know where they are going. Therefore, it is important that the chairman make a concerted effort to ensure that:

Every participant has a clear understanding of the meeting objectives at the start of the meeting.

Each agenda item has a time allocation. The time limit for the meeting should be announced when the agenda is published, or at the beginning of the meeting.

The objective(s) remain valid throughout the meeting. If not, they should be revised.

Meeting objective(s) can be communicated more readily if the chairman does not try to force them on the participants. A consensus about the objectives at the beginning will vastly improve chances for success of the meeting.

Do you play your role well at a meeting? For a meeting to succeed, the chairman must display strong leadership and he and the participants must be willing and determined to:

Become acquainted with each of the participants and carry on a light conversation with them during the "warm-up" session at the beginning of the meeting.

Give the other participants an opportunity to present their ideas, opinions, and recommendations without interrupting or degrading their comments.

Listen wisely and well to the other participants.

Accept new or fresh thoughts and ideas expressed by other participants, provided these thoughts and ideas support the objective(s) of the meeting.

Assist in the process of arriving at a consensus by combining ideas with those of others, reconciling them through compromise, or coordinating them with other ideas.

Do away with non-relevant issues, perceptions, or personal conjectures as soon as they arise and before they can become disruptive.

Always be patient and flexible (but with caution).

4. Major Problems in Running a Meeting

One of the major problems a group often faces at the beginning of a meeting is reaching agreement on both top-level and sub-level objectives. The objectives must be agreed upon before the meeting proceeds, if it is to be successful.

A second major problem concerns the personalities of participants. For example, the chairman may be dominant/submissive, have a desire to be liked, or want to impress his superiors. On the other hand, the invited participants may be self-centered, talkative/shy, aggressive/defensive, argumentative/unresponsive. The participants may have trouble communicating because of differences in age, rank, expertise, and prestige. The ideas of some participants may be ignored and others ridiculed. The mood of the group may be one of elation, depression, or regression.

There is no way to avoid these personality problems; therefore, the challenge facing the chairman is how to deal with them effectively. The answer is based upon creating an environment for effective communication. The problems can usually be resolved if the participants can communicate with one another. The problems will not be resolved if they remain hidden.

A firmly established, finite time limit for the meeting is the single most effective means of eliminating non-contributory discussion. It gives the group a common purpose and helps the chair- man police inappropriate comments.

Another major problem that groups sometimes face is having participants become lost in the problems they are attempting to solve. When this happens the chairman must take positive action to bring the meeting back on target. He can do this by taking one of the following two courses of action:

Halting the discussion and redirecting the meeting.

Halting the discussion and trying to find out where it is heading. If it is heading in a direction the participants feel is proper, he can allow the discussion to continue where it left off. If the meeting is heading in the wrong direction, he can change the direction.

The latter is preferable. Failure to do anything almost guarantees failure of the meeting. Halting the discussion and redirecting the meeting without providing an opportunity for participants to comment tends to create a debilitating emotional reaction. This might lead to withdrawal of some participants from further discussion, or precipitate aggression. When the participants pause to consider where the discussion is heading, there will be few adverse effects and the progress of the meeting may be enhanced.

A fourth major problem a group might face is how to make a decision at the proper time. If the chairman feels a consensus has been reached, he should cut off further discussion. A decision reached by consensus is the one most likely to be carried into action effectively. Decisions imposed on a minority by the majority of participants, or on the participants by the chairman, are not likely to be lasting or effective.

Groups often fall short in trying to reach decisions. Outside pressures or deadlines tend to foster majority-type or chairman-type decisions. Therefore, it is imperative that the chairman attempt to create an environment to make a consensus easier to obtain. Such an environment develops when each participant is given an opportunity to be heard or to voice an objection. In any case, before the meeting time limit expires the chairman should try to get the participants to agree that a decision is necessary, even if it falls short of unanimity.

5. Coping with Weakness

In order to make meetings more effective, one must be acquainted with the major weaknesses and ways to cope with them. The most common weaknesses of meetings are that they are slow, expensive, tend to produce a leveling effect, or lead to dilution or division of responsibility. Let's take a closer look at each of these weaknesses.

Meetings tend to be a slow way to get things done. They do not lend themselves to quick, decisive actions. One observer of committee meetings stated, "They keep minutes and waste hours." Delays are not always bad. Delays provide time for objective reviews or ideas and development and/or consideration of alternatives. Thus, delays can lead to better decisions. For a meeting to be effective, those with expertise and/or the need for action, should attend. Inviting experts and providing sufficient time to consider alternative solutions to problems increases the cost of a meeting. However, the cost to an organization if the meeting is not held may be far greater.

There is a tendency at meetings to bring the individual thinking of the participants in line

with the average quality of the group's thinking. This leveling effect takes place when a participant begins to think less as an individual and adapts the ideas of other participants. The normal tendency is to accept ideas of the most dominant individual at the meeting although his ideas may not be the best. Leveling is not always undesirable; it tempers unreasonable ideas and curbs autocrats. The chairman should try to curb the leveling tendency. One way to keep a dominating participant in check is to seat him directly to the chairman's right.

The tendency for a decision made at a meeting to dilute or divide responsibility is a serious one. When this happens, weak managers are prone to blame their failures on that decision. Such comments as "I didn't support this approach at the meeting" are used to explain their failure to perform effectively. The chairman must be attuned to decisions that tend to dilute or divide responsibility and find a way to avoid them. All of the participants should be given an opportunity to express their viewpoints before the decision is made.

6. Wrap-up and Follow-up

The most important part of the meeting is its ending. After all information has been presented, all decisions made, all problem solutions found or all conclusions reached, the chairman must summarize and solidify the results. He must review decisions and then perceive any conflicts that might result. He must give those who made a major contribution to the meeting the credit they deserve. If no major decisions were reached, he must emphasize progress made and nail down assignments that will lead to a future decision-type meeting. The chairman must always follow through on his promises to the group; otherwise the participants will have no enthusiasm for participating in a future meeting if called upon to do so, If a meeting is a prologue to action, the epilogue must produce results. When no action follows a meeting, the meeting can be considered a failure. The chairman must never allow himself to think "activity" is the same as "accomplishment."

To translate decisions reached in a meeting into actions, the chairman must conduct the necessary follow-up action. A strategy used by successful chairmen is to:

Plan the follow-up procedure before the meeting;

Adjust the procedure during the meeting; and

Consolidate the procedure after the meeting.

When the chairman follows up on meeting decisions, he demonstrates that meetings can accomplish something. This encourages future participation.

7. Summary

Meetings are an essential management tool. Meetings can improve communications, promote coordination, develop people, and help to get a job done. Poor meetings waste time and resources and discourage people. In preparing for a meeting, the chairman should ensure that the agenda focuses on accomplishment of specific objectives.

From time to time throughout the meeting, the chairman should take a census to determine whether the objectives are still valid. If not, they should be revised.

For a meeting to be successful, it must be supported within the organization and provide a needed decision or produce worthwhile actions. This will not occur unless several weaknesses related to meetings are overcome: their slowness, expense, tendency to create leveling, and tendency to dilute or divide responsibility.

Also, for a meeting to be successful, consideration must be given to the timing, meeting place, seating arrangements, size of room, and visual aids.

The leader of a meeting must have the right

attitude; a well-conceived plan; and the ability to direct (focus), control, motivate, interpret, and moderate the meeting. He must recognize that reaching initial or revised objectives of the meeting, and follow-up after the meeting, are essential to its success.

The value of an effective meeting may be summed up as follows: It serves as the cornerstone for successful team-building and progress within an organization.

www.ingramcontent.com/pod-product-compliance
Lightning Source LLC
Chambersburg PA
CBHW072311170526
45158CB00003BA/1274